THE MAGICIAN'S ASSISTANT

For Alan and Joe

THE MAGICIAN'S ASSISTANT

Alicia Stubbersfield

Frank,
best wishes
Alicia Stubbersfield
Aldeburgh 2000

FLAMBARD

ACKNOWLEDGEMENTS

I am especially grateful to the members of 'Off the Page' and to Joan Diamond, Siri Hansen and Paul Magrs for their advice and support.

Some of these poems have appeared in the following publications: *Envoi, Giant Steps, Hybrid, Inkshed, Lancaster Litfest Anthologies* (1991 and 1993), *Never Bury Poetry, Poetry Business Competition Anthologies* (1990 and 1991), *Off the Shelf Anthology* (Vane Women, 1994), *The Open College of the Arts Creative Writing Manuals: Starting to Write* (Open College of the Arts, Barnsley, 1990, revised 1991) and *The Experience of Poetry* (Open College of the Arts, Barnsley, 1991), *Poetry Now, Poetry Wales, The Rialto, Smoke, Spokes, Tees Valley Writer, Writing Women*.

The front cover design is by Nigel Holgate.

The photograph on the back cover is by Claire McNamee.

Flambard Press wishes to thank Northern Arts for its financial support.

Published in 1994 by Flambard Press
4 Mitchell Avenue, Jesmond, Newcastle upon Tyne NE2 3LA

Typeset by Pandon Press Ltd, Newcastle upon Tyne
in association with Mary Holcroft Veitch
Printed in Great Britain by Cromwell Press, Broughton Gifford,
Melksham, Wiltshire

A CIP catalogue record for this book is available from the British Library
ISBN 1 873226 11 X
©Alicia Stubbersfield 1994

CONTENTS

THE MAGICIAN'S ASSISTANT

Peering round a handful of curtain,
I can see the audience edging past,
finding their itchy seats in the glare
of the chandelier.

Backstage we wait for our music,
for darkness and our circle of light.
He is dressed in black, I wear shiny
spandex cut high in the leg,
purple feathers heavy on my head.

I support the magician exclaiming
at the wonder of his tricks, I hold rabbits
and the trembling dove; climb into the box,
smiling as he cuts me in half.

Later, with sorcerer's fingers he casts spells
over me. Cushioned by satin we make love in his box,
our whispers echoing, the dove fluttering above us.
Gently he pulls scarf after glittering scarf
from my silky cunt.

IN THE CURIOUS ROOM

i.m. Angela Carter

You can enter this room
where dark-red rugs cover polished boards.
Curtains keep out the light,
candle flames sway like dancers.
Your mother's wedding dress hangs
limp as a body swinging from the beam.
It almost fits you, it will always
almost fit you,
stretched across your soft breasts,
your rounded belly.
You feel dewy grass tickle
the soles of your feet.

Two old women take your hands,
begin to dance: you know the steps.
Mascara runs on their crepey cheeks,
wrinkled mouths are wounds
in faces that have known it all.
You're here and they are pleased,
smiling under the chandelier.

Is it Garbo or Lou Lou
leading you to the scarlet sofa?
Her smooth skin is forever in monochrome.
She touches your lips with hers,
your fingers outline her erect cock:
everything is possible.
She hands you the tiny key
the ruby collar bright as a slashed throat.

Angela watches from behind the gilded mirror
sends figs bulging on black plates.
Vatican wine spills from goblets,
metal-tainted, tasting like iron, like blood.

You are safe in this room.
Twelve tigers wait for the caress of your whip,
hungry behind bars, soothed by the faint,
drifting notes of a piano
coaxed by the woman you kiss into words.

Your name is spelt out in the cards,
your name, and his, arranged in a perfect arc.
A trapeze creaks across the ceiling,
the aerialiste somersaults from bar to bar,
suspended for longer than anyone before.
Her wings throb
beating in sudden, sharp light.
You know they are real.

CIRCUS SONGS

The Tight-Rope Walker

I am walking along a high wire,
shiny, narrow wire,
slowly, precariously, towards you.
You in your spangled costume.
I stretch out my arms,
your sequins gleam enticingly.
Fingers splayed, I keep my balance,
but you are moving backwards,
still smiling at me.

Cartwheels

Today I am in scarlet satin,
spinning round the ring,
sawdust on my hands.
Lights shine from my dance
and you are holding balloons.
Your costume is diamond colours.

Today I backflip
and you catch me.

Winter Season

We're packing up this morning,
I fold costumes, satin on top
to cheer me.
You pull up tent pegs,
load wagons, laugh.

Silence hangs in the big top,
a stale smell clings round
my wire, a washing line.
Last night's hoofprints stamp
out a desire for words.
Near our feet,
the pink poodle snuffles.

Your snake earring glitters,
squeezes me and slides off
through the undergrowth,
leaving only a waving of the grass.

MAYBE

The road not taken
leads to another part of the forest
where briar rose needlepoints bramble
and larch curtsey their long branches,
just touching emerald moss.

Snow spirals through a west wind
almost obliterating the yellow bricks
of this path snaking up to the cottage.
My footsteps disappear behind me,
invisible as the past will be.

You are waiting
in our gingerbread house,
reading by a log fire that crackles
and spits like the fleeing witch
shaking out her black cloak.

No stepmothers tap on our door,
no wolves wheedle their way in.
Our quilt is scarlet, maroon, gold,
autumn leaves stitched together
with a spider's fine thread.

We face each other as amnesiacs,
all our stories told on ancient skin.
Gales howl beyond the latched gate,
a golden goose waddles resolutely past.
This is what we have chosen.

A HUNDRED YEARS

Even their voices are soft
as they bring her warm bread
and blackberry jelly that tastes
of earth, sky, the wind
easing under her window frame.

Her room is silk-lined,
the curtains velvet, searched
like her clothes for lost pins,
a hidden needle: someone else's palm
smoothing their surfaces.

Outside everything is sharp,
roses spike over terracotta brick,
brambles prick the leaves of copper beech.
Peacocks call out through the night,
peck grain she throws from her room.

Her maid leaves the door unlocked.
The princess is sixteen years old,
drawn by the faintest memory
up the spiral staircase to a secret
where a key turns and she slips in.

The spinning wheel clicks,
turning faster
than her heart's rhythm.
She lifts the spindle,
it fits her hand.

She strokes dark wood and steel
until the point enters her skin.
The bright meniscus of blood
rests for a moment on her fingertips,
swells and begins to drop:
a red stalactite freezing.

HALLOWEEN VISITORS

Are you struggling for a hundred miles
through thick air, blown along by gusts,
to find my house, my fireside
on that night when souls roam?

We wouldn't notice
as five small boys swish cloaks,
stretch their mouths round luminous teeth.
Paper bats swoop over plates of sandwiches,
sausage rolls, glasses filled with Ribena blood.
Our pumpkin lantern grins,
glowing through mad eyes.

Will you stand in a shadowy corner
observing the grandson named for you?

I wear glow-in-the-dark tights,
take off witchy fingers
to pass round gingerbread,
drink sloe gin: purple and venous.
Boys screech outside, bob for apples.
Joe won't push his face under water,
stands just inside, watching.

Perhaps you will come closer,
stroke a strand of his brown hair
and, light as a half-felt draught sucking
through a window-frame, touch his skin.

THE DROWNING

I hear you call out my name
a hundred times each night
Mary, Mary, Mary.

The mermaid's hair is blue.
She winds it about your neck
pulls you down past the rocks.

You press your body against hers
wrap your legs around that scaly tail
as she laughs into your face.

She is stroking your flesh away.
Skin flies like kite-tails of seaweed
tugged by the tide on to white sand.

Her long fingers clasp your heart
wrench it from behind your ribcage
she throws it up, catches it, throws it again.

Her tongue licks out all your blood
searching those narrow veins
busy in a tangle of arteries.

Your bones are thin as shells.
She sucks them clean, discards them
in a heap at the bottom of the ocean.

I keep my bedroom dark
velvet curtains are always closed
the sea is always breathing on my window.

NUMBERS

Silently I mouth my name,
turning it round my tongue
until the sounds come back.
Numbers are easy, gentian-coloured
here on my arm.
My head is shaved,
black hair dropping on the floor.

You used to take hold of it,
pulling me to you, your lips on mine.
Now this stubble feels like your chin
the next morning.

Cotton is rubbing my skin,
I scratch all day with nails
bitten to ragged ends.
Our bodies smell of sweat, carbolic,
the sharpness of fear.
We do not look up, do not notice
the colour of other people's eyes.

I see you beside the canal walking
towards me along the path's dried earth,
flies massing like mist.
You grasp my hand.

A bell rings:
the young guard is checking,
his torch stains my face and moves on.

TATTOO

Yellow eyes glaring, claws grabbing
at taut leather tethering her,
the kestrel was a convulsion
of russet feathers, her wings
stretched out and floundering.

The falconer's voice murmured,
he held her against his chest,
his body still and quiet:
she pecked wildly at his hand,
at the gauntlet where he placed her.

Trained to the perfect weight for flight,
hungry to come back to him,
naked chicks stashed in his bag.
She would hurl herself into air,
hover with the merest tremble,
dropping onto his wrist.

When we spoke together,
when he turned my face to his,
stroking my breasts,
I shivered into him:
abandoned myself to this vertigo,
giving myself a new face,
falling back into the world.

Now I want tangible pain,
not the dark hood of his silence,
where his eyes look beyond me
for the sudden beating of wings.

Surgical spirit stings my skin,
I watch as the pattern grows.
The tattooist's needle pierces,
stains red and blue.
The pulse in my neck throbs,
flight feathers spanning out,
quivering across my arm.

FOUR POEMS AFTER PAINTINGS BY CHAGALL

Icarus

I sneeze into your arms,
downy feathers float from wings
fixed to your shoulders
by wax thinned over a flame.
You flinch at the sudden heat
as I bind flesh and feathers,
a new skin holding them
coating my anxious fingers.
My nails preen you, pulling
tiny filaments together.

You stand in front of me
like some glorious Gabriel
or the swan, urgent and beautiful,
before Leda gave in.
You lean to kiss me
and we fall onto our quilt.

One day you will soar away,
your body held in a bubble
of rising thermals.
Below I shall be a toy,
an insect disappearing.

When sunlight yellows those wings
to the colour of your hair,
my eyes narrowed and squinting,
when you stretch out your hands,
fingers closed as you push
into the emptiness of air,
I shall not be with you.

Promenade

Behind us the town
becoming nothing but Lego.
Moorland stretches bright green,
darkening at the edges
where an east wind ruffles long grass,
binds my thin dress close to my body.

He holds my right hand,
wide fingers enclosing mine.
With one tug I could be off:
soaring straight up
into northern air
sharp as vinegar on my face,
somersaulting, cartwheeling
over those red roofs.

I am tempted by purple clouds
just before the storm breaks,
by the earthy smell of rain
after a long drought,
or by the sun
like Icarus wanting to touch
that bright topaz of light.

He watches me, grins to himself,
made special by my feet leaving
these peaty fells.
My arm is a kite string:
he's hanging on tight
now the squally weather's starting.

Lovers Above the Town

We could be anywhere stroked by this sun
glancing off white tables, roses scrambling

over brick, scenting the air between us.
An ocean of traffic noise surges, ebbs,

blue as Salford's summer sky or your eyes,
blinking as you explain a vital point,

cigarette smoke inscribing secret words
that disappear before we can catch them.

Two moths agitate wings fragile as petals,
briefly reckless before the day's violet end.

We have thrown our watches into the canal,
guided now by shadows unfurling

across concrete, the moon suspended
above the town like we are.

Double Portrait with Wine Glass

Today I can walk on water,
the canal's slippery surface shines
under my pointy white shoes.
My silk dress is slit to the thigh,
veil thrown back, flowers wired together.

He salutes me in champagne,
climbs on to my shoulders,
tipsy after too much wine.
I feel the weight of him,
thrusting out my hip to balance.

In church I saw a fuchsia angel
flapping above us, hoping for the best.
Vows stuck in my throat like cake crumbs
drying as they fall. He coaxed each whisper
until the priest was satisfied.

Bells rang out concentric circles
disappearing into yellow cloud.
Confetti shivered over us
as we walked away from everyone
towards the white sports car.

His scarlet jacket is open,
he giggles foolishly, covering
my right eye with his warm palm.
I squint at the photographer
who kneels before us focussing.

This is how we will always be,
framed on our polished sideboard,
smiling at different angles,
minarets glittering behind us,
the water solid as green glass.

A MIRACLE

after Colin Wilbourn's sculpture 'The Upper Room'

In 'The Upper Room' gaps narrow.
It's all a trick of the light
as the table becomes a miracle
of bread and wine placed just so.

You spend ages explaining where
I ought to sit, the point I ought
to begin from
but somehow it doesn't quite work.

Perhaps it's short-sight, astigmatism,
being slightly too small
for this hollowed-out throne
that stops pieces jigsawing together.

Shadows stay shadows,
wicker edges refuse to join.
You walk away, leaving me to screw up
one eye, tilt my head this way and that.

Beside me the river is silky,
reflecting your body crouching
to scud a stone across its green skin.
One, two, three bounces erupt into widening rings.

I push myself back into the tree's warmth,
stretch my spine, one hand cups my right eye:
wooden pillars shift, bricks slot into place.
The last supper laid out on cream linen,

lit by evening sun slanting through narrow
windows draped with ivy and passion flower.
Perfect for a second before clouds quiver over,
shadows settle into cracks and I hear you call.

LOVE ON THE ARK

Noah didn't notice, nor did anyone else,
lost in the thud of hooves, pattering paws,
the struggle to count each pair coaxed in.
Below deck the stench was hot and yeasty,
tigers jostling with lions, tortoises creeping
away from elephants wedged against the wooden wall.
Two giraffes stuck their heads through special holes
flinching as rain struck, closing huge eyes
against wind tipping the boat this way and that.

Shem crouched alone, wrapped a blanket
round his shoulders, tiring of endless grey
split only by lightning, blurred by more rain.
The others were on deck listening to his father
tell another story straight from God.

So no-one noticed a little peahen on her own
quietly preening her chest, watching two peacocks
swish up their tails.
A vestige of light tinselled their feathers,
hundreds of eyes gazed into hundreds of eyes.
Electric-blue necks entwined, trembling among
the shit, the vomit, the queasy and despondent
creatures on that ship.

Later three birds huddled together
like a discarded evening dress in the bedroom corner,
faint moonlight catching sequins now and then,
the scent of warm flesh still inside.

THE MISSES HAVISHAM HAVE A PARTY

Such a swishing of satin and old net,
white heels tapping along polished floors.
Withered bouquets are discarded in corners,
abandoned on the peachy tablecloth, leaving hands
free to juggle with glass and plate.

No-one knows who had the idea, who sent
the invitations or even why brides finally pat
cobwebs into lacy snoods and come along.
A red carpet muffles the stone steps and it is
really just like a wedding except for the lack
of a groom or maids or guests in fine hats.

Each dress seems a little too big, gaping
here and there after all those years pining,
waiting for the nightmare to wind back, play again
a different end with bells ringing, stars glittering,
hope stitched with every bugle bead and pearl button.

Corks cough discreetly, liberating bubbles
to prick the ladies' soft skin.
Several throw back their veils, rip holes
in lace frilled by nibbling mice:
voices rasp like rusted hinges opened
suddenly by the child who's found her secret garden.

Sounds flower into a huge dahlia
of women laughing, cackling, telling stories:
the past's dust shakes out into June sunlight.
None settles on icing drapery, flounced
over tiers and tiers of fruitcake.

One single figure is placed right at the top.
Dressed in white, she smiles a pert
fuchsia-lipsticked smile to herself
as she leans forward, arms stuck out,
ready to fly straight off that cake.

LADY MACBETH

Ice hardens around the castle, freezing the moat,
sending swans away to scavenge by kitchen doors,
ungainly waddling, feathers roughed up by wind.
At night she hears something splintering.

Dawn comes pink across her blank expanse of fields,
she gazes out through the window's narrow slit
still expecting to see him ride over the hillside:
hooves printing out his journey's end.

Under opaque ice is a king's body, upright,
pierced by daggers until dark roses bud from his ribs.
He is waiting for her to pluck the petals
and scatter them over snow's whiteness.

Often another man comes to her saying he is king now
and she is queen, undressing her, touching her all over.
She half-remembers him but his hands are too hot,
she will set on fire, will melt the king's pale skin.

Afterwards she leans out over the sill,
gasps frozen air, washes his smell from her hands.
When she comes to the real king, when it is time for her,
he will not taste of anything but the purity of water.

He is the lover she dreamed of as a girl, waiting
for the first thaw to let crocuses purple the fields.
In her sleep she feels a slow cracking,
surrenders to the recklessness of rain.

DESDEMONA

Moonlight shudders through wooden slats,
seeping down the marble floor:
she can just glimpse the north star.

Emilia is making the bed with linen sheets
warmed by their bodies only nights ago.
On the table stands a vase of lilies.

As she unplaits heavy snakes of hair,
Desdemona watches it fall on her shoulders,
slowly she begins to brush.

She remembers him lifting her onto the bed,
the weight of him moving above her,
his smooth, dark skin.

Yellow as the candle's glimmer, pollen
drops on her nightgown, staining cotton,
staining her fingers.

She scatters the sheets with dried flowers.
Primrose, violet, heartsease
in tiny bruises.

On her knees she prays for him, for herself,
and for their lives leaking through
the words he will not hear.

OPHELIA

His voice is the heaviness of stones in your hem,
slivers of ice spitting at your cheek.
Your tears are daisies, too small to thread,
withering where they fall.

You wear black for him,
an endless pool of taffeta soaking up light.
Your skirt tilts the long grass,
is mottled by dew as you walk.

Columbine veils your bright hair,
fennel seeds take away the bile
rising in your throat,
pansies shred and stick to damp flesh.

Here is the cross he gave you that night,
its crystal brilliant in candle flame.
How heavy it is, how cold against your skin,
cold as this glassy stream.

You bend at the water's edge,
your face wrinkles into an old woman.
He is telling you to slip
under those cool white sheets,

to slide your arms down the satin sleeves
of the leopard coat he brought,
its collar making your face tiny.
Let him warm you now before it is too late.

A circus of lapwings tumble overhead,
two curlews glide their cries up and up,
taking him with them, beyond you, out of reach.
You can turn around, change your mind, run away.

SAPPHO LEAPS INTO THE SEA

These cliffs are sharp as shoulder blades, are
abandoned to the sun. You come dressed in black,
brambles tear your skirts, scratch at your legs,
still you scramble upwards.
Beside the track rocks tumble like skulls,
dust catches in your throat, retch it away,
there is no water here.
You stop, eat blackberries
until your mouth is purple.
Suddenly you see her
standing just up the track.
She is laughing, her hair blows against her face.
It is how you first saw her.
Your voice is trapped somewhere behind rocks,
she can't hear you.
In her arms there are flowers, oleander, jasmine,
darkness mixes with the smell of the sea.

You are at the cliff's rim.
You hear her whispering, it isn't your name
she sighs, cries out. You remember the taste of her.
Sea and sky are whirling
with jasmine and oleander,
one step: your body's star
spins into the vortex
of its last scream.

TULIPS FOR SYLVIA

I see you in your study,
scarlet corduroy curtains,
red Wilton stretched over floorboards.
The inside of a Valentine,
a raw heart pulsing in someone's palm.

Snow quilts a grave's open wound.
Yours is in the corner:
I kneel, plant my votive candle,
its small flame striving.
Hughes has been ripped away,
the scar softened by more snow.
You are bone, still incandescent,
wrapped at last in earth's warmth.

Your husband brings home a rabbit,
ready to skin, gut, prepare for you
to cook with wine and garlic,
rosemary scenting all the kitchen.
He will sit opposite you eating this food,
touch your hand resting on the table,
get up and kiss the nape of your neck.

Wax seeps down the candle,
making a pale scab,
snow begins to obliterate my tulips,
their petals like little rags of skin.
I must struggle back, bend against the hillside,
disappear into this vortex of snow.

PHEASANT

Today winter has begun our slow
shrivelling into houses and coats,
wrapped away from the wind's edge.
Rooks cough in the beech,
jackdaws whirling into a pale sky.

She sits at her table writing letters.
Outside, yellowing grass almost hides
the pheasant stalking her garden:
scarlet head bobbing, eye bold and dark,
breast feathers bronzed by a weak sun.

On the road six Range Rovers drive past,
stuffed with guns, shooting sticks and men
laughing, competing, rehearsing stories.
Birds are brought here, fed and protected;
bright foreigners perched on stone.

Her house is cold, winter slips through gaps,
wraps her shoulders as she bends over the page.
The pheasant gives a warning 'chuck' but he is
staying in her garden: she knows he's there,
brilliant and still surprising.

DECEMBER IN MANCHESTER

Yesterday she was grey cloud, backlit by his fierce sun,
walking in big strides over mud and winter grass.

At the top they leaned on cairnstones,
ate cheese and tomato, the skin full
ready to split against her teeth.
She looked down at sheep, white as gulls,
a rowan tree bloody with fruit.

Outside the pub, sharp beer on her tongue,
she heard the rook's raucous laugh.

Today she hurries with city crowds
along streets grey as pigeons
pecking at last night's vomit
splashed across stone:
the air is yellow bile.

All she sees are her own feet,
black shoes, mud washed away.
Street lights tinsel her face.

The city's wings fold around her,
feathers streaked in black oil.
She feels its claws tighten.

Streetsellers call out, children wail,
the banjo player continues to dance.
She can hear the faint cry
of a curlew
circling high over Crummackdale.

TROUBLESOME HORSES

'The troublesome horse. He is valuable for it is he
that pulls towards the beautiful.' (Simone Weil)

She rode adolescence on horses,
glossy creatures with arched necks,
heads bending into the bridle and her
hands light on the reins.

Muscles strained against the field slope
galloping at hedges and painted jumps:
eyes always on the one ahead,
making sure they met it just right.

She wanted to go faster, leap higher, ride
the bright horse that could throw her
with one sudden twist:
galloping into the storm's cloud.

Now there are no horses to ride
she still looks for the wild one.
A troublesome horse pulling
towards the beautiful

across those ploughed fields,
legs heavy with mud,
hurtling at each dark fence:
they leap into the light.

A SENSE OF PLACE

I am going back to that valley
where the sun slants in,
holding its breath.

I want to walk in the ruined church,
feeling the strong arch of its back,
the safety of its stone floor.

There the dead are with us:
Evelyn, Thomas, Rebecca Jane,
making rich soil under a bleak landscape.

I walk with my father's stride,
looking with his grey eyes beyond faint
mill chimneys and a whisper of woodsmoke.

His lawyer's love of language
gave me garden enough to grow
the dreams of my mother's family:

exiles staring across endless valleys.
In this churchyard moss and lichen
gleam on stone.

FORGET-ME-NOT

Sun is warming limestone's vertebrae,
seeping into dark grykes,
glinting from a spider's web stretched
edge to edge catching petals.

I lie on stone,
hardly touching my spine to rock.
Trapped behind its thin cage
my heart is beating too fast.

I remember you holding eyebright,
stroking back each petal
to show the purple centre
almost hidden away.

There is eyebright here pressing
fragile roots against rock,
sheltering from northern winds:
a speck of silver in rough grass.

You brought me here in autumn,
larch leaves drifting over moss.
Our hands hardly touched, yours strong
as this stone under my back.

Midges cloud overhead biting my skin.
Shadows cross the patch of forget-me-not,
I pick one small flower:
a blue lantern to light me home.

MOVING PLANTS

Magnolia are just past their best,
dropping tongues on our suburban street.
Mock cherry thickens along branches
bending under the weight.

You are moving shrubs in the garden,
preparing new places for them to thrive.
Earth has been riddled and mulched,
warm holes dug for those unravelled roots.

It has taken hours to decide
where to put each one:
you've studied the colour, size,
the exact slant of the sun.

We are moving to Yorkshire,
still tangled in Manchester's black soil.
Ease me out with gentle hands,
find me a view across the hills.

A warm stone house with my own room
where books line the walls,
my desk piled with letters from friends,
above it the painting you gave me.

Put me on the edge of the moors,
limestone outcrop set like bone.
There I can lean into the wind,
a hawthorn tree clinging on.

WATERFALL AT WEST BURTON

We bite wild garlic leaves,
keep their heat on our tongues for ages.
Creamy flowers spangle the high sides
of this limestone grotto where swifts
hurtling overhead are tiny Tornadoes,
their noise sucked into the waterfall's
insistent jazz.

You stride off across slippery rock
towards water that drops and froths,
speeding the beck under an arched bridge,
past the ducks' nest and the drooping fern.
Stone curves inwards dimming afternoon light,
makes us hunch over until we reach the edge.

Hennaed water zigzags past us
becoming a Bridget Riley painting,
the dizzying vertigo of suicides on Beachy Head,
trains roaring over the viaduct in *Cabaret*
and you like Sally Bowles screaming under it,
your hair heavy with spray,
darkened to the colour of this water,
to the colour of Laphroaig.

Faces stinging we turn back,
walk the marked footpath over grass softened
by lambs almost old enough to leave.
Deepened by nights of rain
the river is Guinness now and slower,
restrained by bends, fallen trees, a half-built weir.
We can still hear the waterfall's raucous music,
soon the river will pass through larch woods
hurrying to make that first fabulous leap into space.

ENLARGING THE HEART

'… happiness is increased not by the enlargement of the
possessions, but of the heart…'   (John Ruskin)

Coniston Water curls and stretches,
blue air colours Brantwood, the fells, me
sitting outside eating avocado and warm bread,
writing a postcard, 'drinking lemon tea
reminds me of you, of the last time…'
My skin is touched by this light
not thrush-egg or cerulean but gentian
hazing a veil over everything.

Up the hill, Ruskin's house lives
filled again with paintings, books,
his collection of shells, pieces of stone.
Huge windows frame the view
for crowds of visitors stopped by this man
who believed, *There is no wealth but life.*
Yet couldn't make love to anyone.

At the lake I step onto the ferry,
sit on polished wood, holding an edge
worn smooth by seventy years of hands.
The boat's old engine thrums
pushing it through choppy waters.
Looking down I see nothing,
no eels, no glimpse of Campbell's *Bluebird*
rusting somewhere beneath us.

Waves tilt the boat, shake my heart.
I think of you soothing it in your cupped hands
making blue flesh pink again,
pink and plumped up like a pillow.

LIKE HONEY

I unwrap the hours before I see you
like purple foil from Cadbury's chocolate,
slowly, anticipating each sweet mouthful.

Desire for you fills the air with scents
of rosemary, French cigarettes, cut lemon.
It runs like honey between my ribs,
leaves me sticky:

whispers 'This time, this time.'
Behind my eyes
I'm listening.

OLD WINE

Across the red-and-white tablecloth
their elbows meet,
too bony for comfort.
Plates of lasagne distract
the meeting of eyes,
and flickering of candles.

Half-filled with old wine,
their glasses circle the table:
never quite catching the light.

THE HOCKNEY EXHIBITION, SALT'S MILL

Everywhere the sweet corruption of lilies,
speckled hot pink, stamens snuggled in.
Paintings jumble above our heads or hang
in measured distances, one lies in a wheelbarrow
scented with French lavender.

It is a friend's front room, his piano,
his table strewn with paperbacks and postcards,
drawings of Celia slumped in a seventies dress,
unbuttoned as I was in Ossie's black crepe
twenty years ago when Cheltenham was my California.

Verdi unspools on my skin, quickening with my breath
and searing some secret place
before falling in circles
on blue water that cools slowly under the sun's weight.
My chair's thin metal presses each vertebra.

Soon you come to meet me and we drink coffee beside
Hockney's holiday snaps of a Yorkshire brighter
than mine where sheep gleam on brilliant hills.
Even sugar is rainbow in this place, melting just the same
though I can conjure its honey weeks later.

LOVE IS NOT CONSOLATION

It is sharp as arc-lights burnishing wire,
marking a perimeter that's not fixed.
I freeze in its sudden cold: blind, blinking
till my pupils narrow and I see again,
never so clearly as I did before.
Now everything becomes insubstantial,
candlelit, shadows are growing monstrous
or tiny: our faces in soft-focus.
These are magic candles from a child's cake.
I lick my fingers, try to stub them out,
sparks sizzle and hiss, spurt, steady again,
burning despite draughts that spit like tomcats.

Love is not consolation, it is light:
the hall lamp left on during a long night.

SOMEONE ELSE'S BOOKS

You had a hangover
but we went to the bookshop anyway.
Dust spiralled through tired sunlight,
settling in our hair, on yellowed pages.
We squatted to reach low shelves,
walked sideways trying to remember
some author's name, reading the sexy bits
out to each other, giggling in little rooms.

I found books belonging to someone I once knew,
inscriptions in her curved writing,
For Malcolm and all the firsts we've had,
and his to her,
Christmas 1972, for Morag, with all my love.
Two lives measured through their reading,
private times abandoned for unravelling.

My rooms are peopled with books,
some battered, conjuring me as a child,
my mother asking who I was today,
always not quite here, caught in a story.
These books will end up in a shop too,
stippled with grit, chucked in boxes,
strangers touching their covers,
reading my secrets and imagining my life.

You felt sick but didn't say so,
I was dizzy from stretching for first editions.
Downstairs you paid for *Arabian Nights*,
the assistant's red nails scraping your palm.
Outside you held your book like a talisman
against the curdled sky.

MOONRISE

Don't send me photographs of the moon,
shadows burned into unthinkable brightness.
I might imagine myself there again, mouth full
of hope, my body still molten under white light.

I would want to stand at midnight on that beach
warmed all day by a sun too hot to move in;
throw pebbles at the trail glossing black water,
watching them bounce twice and then sink.

A slow wind would be endlessly rummaging,
shifting clouds across pale sky:
nightjars forever commenting on the lovers
dizzied by stars, by breath aching behind ribs.

Lose the negatives in the back of a drawer,
a stiff roll gathering scratches and dust.
You'll come upon them, each frame held
against the light until my face blurs into view.

BLACKBERRIES

For days rain had drizzled darkness
into her house: water foamed across tracks,
her feet sank as she filled bags,
blackberries squashed against plastic.
Carrying them home, wild scent on her skin,
she dreamed of juice oozing from sugary crusts.

The fire was out. She raked ashes and swept,
dust settled in her hair, soured her mouth.
He would be on the motorway now, driving
towards her, expecting warmth saved up all week.
Tipping berries into the sink, she squeezed them
through her hands, made the water pink.

His key clicked in the lock, she turned to face him:
fingers dripping and no fire lit.

LETTERS FROM GREECE

Manchester

A letter came almost every day,
blue envelopes, pieces of Greek sky.
She didn't want them
staring at her
as she eased open her front door:
his black ink weaving her back in.
Thin paper crackled in her fingers,
his certain voice threaded each word,
conjuring sea sounds, limestone cliffs
edging down to turquoise water.
Outside her window, Manchester
breathed its own darkness.

Agios Petros

His room was cool, light arrowed through
dark shutters, cigarette smoke drifting
past the resin smell of pine and salt.
Lying on the hard bed, he creased cotton sheets,
heard the cicadas rasp.
Arum lilies grew in clumps by the road,
pale swathes of rosemary bordered the villa.
He crushed green spikes,
keeping the scent all day.
That night he wrote to her,
slept hardly at all,
woke sticky with memory's sweat.

Painting Things White

After work she bought cans of paint,
white-out of bedroom walls,
Liberty print blanked into bone.
His absence glittered, her arms ached.
The moon was on its back
making shadows in a green light.
Later she drank gin, ice clinking,
a blue letter crumpled in her hand.
Tomorrow there'd be another
roping her to him:
she flattened to his shape,
longing for his mouth.

Through His Lens

Through his camera lens he changed the world,
perfecting shades of light and dark,
storks high in crazy nests, bats skating
against a moon-striped sky.
He photographed lizards half-hidden
behind rock, a wild gleam of green,
stones that were marbled and sea-moist.
Oiled evenings slipped past him,
warm air wrapped his darkening shoulders.
He shrugged away the thought of her
spent hours developing an exact image,
sent her the contact prints.

An Unusually Hot June

Heat sent her out of Manchester
drawn by hills, light glittering on water.
Lunch outside a pub, summer called up
by rosebay willowherb spiking down banks,
The Beach Boys blaring from rusty cars.
Sun stroked her neck, left a shadow
on the letter she was writing,
freckles smudging her arms.
Lying down, her spine against stone,
only blue sky
and swifts circling,
soaring into the hills.

Waiting

The day before she came he visited a church
anchored half-way up the mountain path.
In the garden, oleander heavy as incense,
butterflies sucking each pink flower:
whitewashed walls burned under his hand.
Inside a woman cradled one candle,
its flame yellowing her face.
Painted stars glowed on the ceiling,
light spilled through coloured glass.
He left without a photograph,
counting stone steps and the hours
before he would see her.

On the Back of the Bike

On the second day they hired a motor-bike:
he would show her tiny clots of villages,
neat olive groves stepping up hillsides,
and the place where Sappho,
staring into dizzying sea, decided to jump.
She settled behind him, tightened her thighs,
wound his T-shirt's soft cotton in her fingers.
They leaned into corners, waved at Greeks
smiling from doorways and dusty tavernas,
felt the engine's pull, up and up,
winding into mountains: all the time, warm air
on her face, her heart beating against his back.

Summer Is Over

Straight-necked geese flew over Manchester,
their cries disappearing into lowering cloud.
Blackberries scabbed grimy hedges,
swifts flexed wing muscles swirling together.
She folded summer clothes, threw away Ambre Solaire.
His first card came from the Pindos Mountains,
the second from the Italian Alps:
each one signed 'See you soon.'
Pruning roses, she smelled November
coming in across the grass.
She saved one scented flower to take inside,
cutting the rest right back.

MARIO

Mario cooks fish with fennel:
slicing a clean line, flesh opening
like a lip, he pulls away the tangle
of guts, washes blood away.

Grilling slowly, the skin
is charred to splitting.
He has chosen from the night's catch,
weighing each body in his hands.

Heat sweats into every corner
of his village but Mario sits
under an olive tree mending nets;
tying tiny knots, stitching threads
together ready for evening.

Soon he will go back to Milano:
his broad hands holding books
instead of fish, diagnosing those
strange surfaces of human skin.

His boat slips away from the quay
following the moon's slow trail.
A light bobs behind, drawing fish
into nets where their bodies writhe.

Dawn turns the Calabrese mountains pink,
light reflecting from hospital windows;
Mario waits for the baby's head,
his hands ready as she struggles out,
gasping her first cold mouthful of air.

THROUGH THE FISH-EYE MIRROR

He was dark and drank his melancholy
like Guinness, a surface froth of love.
She sang brightly at him,
sharp and edgy as ice.

They sat together in a corner
where music played and people laughed.
A birthday seemed to be going on,
cake crumbs and too many candles:
a photographer stilled the action.

Her red nails tapped the table,
he sat with arms folded
until alcohol moved him and she
laughed into his eyes
where he held her.

Time was called: they shifted in their seats
reluctant to leave the warmth.
The pub's brass glow reflecting their faces
like a fish-eye mirror.

Wound round each other, they pushed outside
into the afternoon's dreary sea-light.
Shoppers darted past, phosphorescent
under the streetlamps.

He gazed at her, promising a phonecall,
hunched into his mac and walked away.
She wrapped a scarf round her shoulders,
dropped the shredded beer mat,
piece by piece,
into the gutter.

FEBRUARY 14TH AT THE CLINIC

Instruments glinted in quiet rows,
the doctor smoothed his new green gloves.
His patient lay on leatherette and waited,
her knees pointing like stars.

In town he walked past shops full of hearts:
carried chocolate to melt her searching tongue,
found slippery satin to smudge her red lips,
a bunch of roses with all their thorns cut off.

It was nearly lunchtime, she was the last,
the speculum slid in, deliberate as her breath.
She watched trees bend outside the window,
caught her throat at sudden pain.

Her flowers were wrapped in pink paper,
their petals bruising against his chest.
The doctor's fingers pressed her skin's bud,
left a heart-shaped stain spreading.

THE TEST

Squatting over the bowl she peed into
a perspex jar, splashing her hand.
She put the kit on her windowsill,
watched snow slip down the glass.
Sodium lights glowing yellow
spotted by black flakes.

He had stroked her stomach, imagining
its gradual ripening under his hands:
she tightened her belly
wanting that slow creep of red.

His words vibrated round her
but a hundred miles from him
she would sluice away
the clotting mass of cells.
He turned back; she drove off,
headlights cutting into mist.

At the clinic protesters shouted, made her
push through rosaries, pictures of scarlet
embryos curled like prawns.
In his room he spread out their photographs,
taken too long ago, the focus hazy:
he began to tear them.

Drowsy with anaesthetic she touched herself,
skin stretched over jutting bones.
Her mouth was dry she tried to wet
cracked lips with her tongue.
No-one would come:
nothing but the heat
of her own blood.

A KIND OF SICKNESS

Each night in her dreams she is vomiting,
heaving up gushes of liquid that splash down steps,
over theatre balconies, into plates at parties.
Now and then it's blood, bright and arterial,
clotting as it lands, or just dry retching:
her whole body shaken awake.

Nightmares darken her eyes as she makes breakfast,
sends the children upstairs to wash, dress for school.
Her husband drinks coffee from French china,
strokes her arm as she leans across the table.
He'll be late again, driving home through unlit lanes,
dodging hedgehogs that struggle in the headlight's glare.

Days lengthen as she waits for him, keeping food hot,
taking the boy to football, the girl to piano,
chatting at the school gates about reading and spelling,
the decline in self-control: children come out screaming.
From six o'clock, wine is enough to ease her mouth,
to welcome him smiling through kitchen steam.

In bed he is beside her, eyelids fluttering, his hand
rests on her thigh but she's already dreaming.
Bodies pile up by the roadside, wounds begin to congeal,
blood slips across tarmac, her feet are sliding,
mouth full of bile, arms outstretched and waving.
She's running downhill, faster and faster, towards someone.

LETTERS

That evening the swallows came back,
searching out old nests,
swooping round her house
in an ecstasy of recognition.
One perched on the telegraph wire,
gunmetal blue, a red patch
glistening at its throat.

She stood in the garden,
blossom frothing her hedge,
night air smelling of grass
and recent rain:
its green filled her up,
her fingers touching the letter
folded in her pocket.

He said he was alive,
missing her and taking care
in the desert's interminable heat.
She searched black ink for clues,
wanting more of him:
her hand closed into a fist.

Rain began again,
slow drops spattering her face.
She stayed still, listening
to a cuckoo's last call
drift into the failing light.

AFTER THE ACCIDENT

You phone and tell me you are not dead,
not blown to pieces by an Iraqi bomb
on the underground where I imagine your blood,
redder than anyone else's, splattered over tiles.

You tell me about the bike sliding on ice
black as tarmac, black as your leather jacket,
about falling, smelling petrol spilled on the road:
a rainbow to catch the stars' cold gleam.

You speak across fields smeared with fog.
I move around the house, put coal on the fire,
listen again to war reports on the radio,
and have to turn it off.

In the orchard, crocus begin to push through
iron-fisted earth, yellow and purple bruises will
fade from your skin. I shall arrive on your doorstep,
my arms full of flowers, strewing petals behind me.

SAFE

Since he came home he has not touched me,
just watched with eyes empty as a mirror;
my body reflected in the blank surface.
Whispering love, sitting opposite,
he is letting me drift on his memory's raft.

I lie waiting for his arms to pull me
back into the warmth of him: too much
sun has bleached our quilt, colours
fading into each other, the pattern dulled.
Bits of my clothes, and his, stitched in.

Sometimes the nightmares start; huddled
at the bed's edge he screams and sobs.
I try to soothe him, a warm sponge
touching scorched skin, he wants ice:
walking narrow streets in any weather.

Once I searched his case, found photographs
of young men with limbs shot away;
letters from me, a piece of frayed
green cloth, black hair wound into a knot.
I put them all back: didn't say anything.

I wonder at those returned in bags,
hopes zipped out of sight, their women
allowed to mourn: I should wear black,
should take anemones to his grave
and leave them there.

THE DAY IRAQ INVADED KUWAIT

Heat veiled Widdop Moor, polishing the reservoir
into stillness. Gritstone squatted in heather:
dinosaur silhouettes, waiting.
He carried pink rope coiled over his shoulder,
she walked slowly, already feeling sweat prickle,
watching gulls circling, dropping
like silence behind rock.

Harnessed to her he began to climb,
she was ballast, keeping the rope
until he was there, calling to her,
words fluttering into her fear.

Burnt grass stretched like sand
down to the water, sun scalded her.
Grasping at rock tore her fingernails,
still his voice echoed, talking her up.
She hated him, hated the ground falling away,
the tightness of rope holding her.

She did it: could almost touch a swift
curving past, was able to see where he pointed.
Far beyond them to the horizon hazed across land
shaken by tanks, by planes
that had thundered over these crags.

She turned to him, their bodies haloed
in light that cast shadows across rock
shifting under them.

A FLOWER FOR KURDISTAN

*Jasmine is the Kurds' national flower and is believed
to have the properties of an aphrodisiac.*

Jasmine shivers against Yorkshire stone,
wind chilling down from northern hills.
Tendrils reach out,
clutching at the walls of his house.

She held his hand scrambling upwards,
following an old path into woods
where water feathered past,
gathering itself to spill over stones.

They smelt jasmine before they saw it,
thick, heady and sweet,
breathed its perfume before tasting
the salt of each other's skin.

This year buds are blackened
by a late frost, no flowers opening,
no aromatic scent warming clear air:
only clogged roots still stirring.

He watches people die in another country,
their eyes dreaming home.
Heavy boots turn footprints into mud:
disturb the stench of something rotting.

WOMEN IN THE DESERT

Sand muffles everything: voices whisper across
ribs of it, boots catch in impossible softness.
Grit under the lids has dried up my eyes,
I suck water all day, still don't sweat.
Only mosquitoes whine through this night air:
we are waiting, a rifle heavy over my arm.
War has not scared me, my body lean, hair short;
I smear earth colours on my face until
a stranger rises in my mirror.
I run like a man, screech as the bayonet enters.
Behind the gun my eye is true,
I hit the target over and over.
Cloud streaks the moon: remembering
old rhythms of pain and blood,
my womb contracts letting in the dark.

Wind ruffles sand over our footprints,
buries all trace of us.

ARAB NECKLACE IN A SELLING EXHIBITION

Beads spill into my hand, three
thousand years old, light as bone.
Turquoise threaded with terracotta stars,
cataracts of lapis preserved in sand.

Jewellery that circled a girl's neck,
her name etched on one tiny stone.
Warm winds rumpled dunes over her,
filled her eyes, stopped her ears.

Identity tag from a desert rumbling
with guns, tanks flattening sand.
Oil burns against a sky scarred by
vapour trails curving behind planes.

Her amulet clatters on the counter:
blue and rust held by a snake clasp.
I wind its dryness round my throat,
soaking up my mind's terrible heat.

1931

Two straw-hatted girls hold hands and dolls,
looking out to a hard white sun
beating on whiter square houses
and a dust-blown track.
Inside is cool, dark and quiet:
a Bergère chair rocks, the mahogany clock
sounds out the silky hours until dusk.
Pictures of camels stand above blue vases,
A Persian rug stretches on the floor.
A dark woman smooths her hair,
walks through a bamboo curtain
to where the girls play.

In cafés, men sit talking of war.
Englishmen drinking aniseed, eating olives,
spitting out passion's hard stones.

Dust blows down the track,
girls kiss their donkey goodbye
and are afraid of the journey.
Wrapped and tied, they travel,
bundling along in trains to Lisbon,
onto a cargo ship.
The dark woman tries to laugh,
is photographed against green waves
and neat white rails.

Liverpool: fine pencil lines of drizzle
shade grey into their eyes.
Warehouses stare down blankly at the gap
where a black car glides.
Two little girls pull on woolly hats,
looking out at rows of houses marching
interminably towards some dark centre.

Their mother huddles into a fur collar,
draws the purple coat tight against her:
plays with a long, cold key.

G.I. BRIDE

A bungalow squats on the town's edge,
away from grimy streets
but dusted with the colliery soot
of lost northern dreams.

The daughter has shining hair and a fine waist:
she laughs, smooths lobelia crepe,
adjusts a veil more rakishly over her eyes.
Her gloves could be made of fish skin.

She steps out and into his arms.
The American officer spins her
across pitted dance floors, along narrow streets,
colouring her days with Hollywood.

Her ticket arrives. The ship is white
like the wedding dress and her mother's tears.

BETWEEN CORFU AND ALBANIA

His little boat slipped away
from Albania's raw cliffs,
pushing into darkness
and the forbidden sea to Greece.
Cicadas were almost silent,
their daytime tinnitus stilled.
Water sucked limestone rocks,
a sudden wind stirring the waves.

Behind him were closed doors,
shuttered windows, bottles full
of the red wine he drank all year
while listening to tourists' cries,
watching packed boats dawdle past,
bright flags taunting the thin coast.

Across the channel, widowed in black net,
olive trees twist, turning from the light
dappling white pebbles.
The sea rattles stone against stone,
touching and drawing back.

She hoses down the dusty taverna,
ready for visitors who will soon
mark out territories on the small beach.
By lunchtime the caiques are tied-up,
waiting for people laughing, spending money.
She tries not to remember the dull thudding
of his flesh washed up by that spring tide.

THE LAST POST

The coffin was smaller than she expected:
pale wood, fine grained, warm to her touch.
She stared at it for a long time unable
to imagine his body hardening inside.

Their leaving had been a forties film,
cameras lingered on women saying goodbye:
her fingers touching his neck, his hands
clasped, for a moment, round hers.

Sea lurched against the quayside mixing
brown froth with litter and yellowed leaves.
His uniform blurred into the grey
of other men clamouring aboard.

At home she pushed open the silence,
let television news fills her room;
a politician's mouth salting the wound
of their last kiss.

When they told her she said nothing,
wandered round the house closing curtains.
Rain splattered against windows,
making tracks through the dust.

His coffin was lowered into crumbling soil,
a cold handful rattling the lid:
seagulls screeched overhead, disappearing
into cloud and the bugle's last note.

New Titles from Flambard

PETER BENNET: *All the Real*

ANDREA CAPES: *Home Fires*

CYNTHIA FULLER: *Moving Towards Light*

ANNA KAMIENSKA: *Two Darknesses*

SHEONA LODGE: *Swan Feather*

PETER MORTIMER: *A Rainbow in its Throat*

CHRISTOPHER PILLING: *Foreign Bodies*

PATRICIA POGSON: *The Tides in the Basin*

MICHAEL STANDEN: *Months and other stories*

MICHAEL STANDEN: *Time's Fly-Past*

ALICIA STUBBERSFIELD: *The Magician's Assistant*

FLAMBARD NEW POETS 1: *Annie Foster, Fiona Hall, Caroline Smith*

Distributed by Password (Books) Ltd,
23 New Mount Street, Manchester M4 4DE.